Fire & Flood Study Guide

FIRE& FLOOD
STUDY GUIDE

Digging for Truth
in an Age
of Deception

LYNNETTE FIELD &
DAWN MORRIS

NASHVILLE

NEW YORK • LONDON • MELBOURNE • VANCOUVER

FIRE & FLOOD STUDY GUIDE

Digging for Truth in an Age of Deception

Published in New York, New York, by Morgan James Publishing. Morgan James is a trademark of Morgan James, LLC. www.MorganJamesPublishing.com

Scripture quotations taken from the (NASB®) New American Standard Bible®, Copyright © 1960, 1971, 1977, 1995, 2020 by the Lockman Foundation. Used by permission. All rights reserved. www.lockman.org.

To order additional books:
www.amazon.com
www.dawn-morris.com

Proudly distributed by Ingram Publisher Services.

Morgan James BOGO™

A **FREE** ebook edition is available for you or a friend with the purchase of this print book.

_____

CLEARLY SIGN YOUR NAME ABOVE

Instructions to claim your free ebook edition:
1. Visit MorganJamesBOGO.com
2. Sign your name CLEARLY in the space above
3. Complete the form and submit a photo of this entire page
4. You or your friend can download the ebook to your preferred device

ISBN 9781636980195 paperback
ISBN 9781636980201 ebook
Library of Congress Control Number:
2022942943

Cover Design by:
Rachel Lopez
www.r2cdesign.com

Interior Design by:
Chris Treccani
www.3dogcreative.net

Morgan James is a proud partner of Habitat for Humanity Peninsula and Greater Williamsburg. Partners in building since 2006.

Get involved today! Visit MorganJamesPublishing.com/giving-back

Table of Contents

A Note from the Authors

Fire & Flood is a fictional novel based on events past and future in the Bible. While the story is engaging and exciting, the book is meant to make you THINK! *What do you know about major events recorded in the Bible? Why is it important to know what the Bible says—even if you're not sure you believe in God!?*

Did you know there is one book in the Bible that says, "READ ME, I'M SPECIAL?" This same book promises a SPECIAL BLESSING to anyone who reads it and heeds what it says. We don't know about you, but both of us want *every* blessing God offers us. He promises a particular blessing for those who will study the Book of Revelation: "Blessed is he who reads and those who hear the words of the prophecy and heed the things which are written in it; for the time is near" (Revelation 1:3).

No matter what your thinking about future events may be, it's our hope that you will open the Bible with an open mind and keep the following "Golden Rule" in mind, even as you're looking at the book of Revelation: "When the plain sense of Scripture makes common sense, seek no other sense, lest it result in nonsense." (David L. Cooper)

We also strongly recommend that you *pray* before discussing the questions in this study guide, asking God for His wisdom. It is our great hope that this guide would inspire you to continue seeking out God's infallible truth, and to:

- always seek the Bible as your first resource
- see what other credible sources say…

- and then go back to the Bible, and make sure it checks out!

By the end of this study, we pray you will
learn,
grow,
and fall deeper in love
with the King of Kings who made you,
loves you, and gave His only Son to save YOU!

Lynnette Field and Dawn Morris

How to Find Bible Verses

Each book of the Bible may be easily found using the Table of Contents, found in the front of the Bible. There are 66 books in both the Old and New Testaments.

Below is an example of the parts of a Bible verse:

Revelation 21:1
Book; Chapter; Verse

For a more thorough explanation, see: https://www.wikihow.com/Look-up-a-Bible-Verse

Study Guide Overview

You will find the chapter studies in this guide arranged as follows:

I. Looking at the Book (*Fire & Flood*):

In this section you will find questions pertaining to things said and done by the characters; it is a surface study. In other words, "What was going on in this chapter? Did we really read THAT?!"

II. Looking at the Bible:

These Bible passages are provided so you can read for yourself what God has said in His Word about topics raised in the book. The Bible is our guiding light to clear things up, and for real help and great wisdom!

III. Looking at Ourselves:

Here we will examine how the idea or message in the chapter applies to each person's individual life, and how you can use what you've learned to help yourself and others, and/or to make a difference in the world around you.

Because there are 48 short chapters in this novel, with a wide range of discussion topics, it is recommended that the chapters be divided into the number of weeks available for the study. For example, if a group allotted eight weeks for this book study, each week would cover six chapters.

If it were a 16-week study, the first and last meeting might cover the introduction and conclusion, covering four chapters per meeting, and providing some flexibility for lengthier discussions.

This study guide is meant to be a resource to encourage you to study and learn from the Bible, which is God's Word to us. If we read the Scriptures, and hold to God's teachings, He promises to give us wisdom and understanding (Proverbs 2).

If you are a leader of a group study, please feel free to pick and choose whatever questions might interest you and your group. Don't feel like you have to use every question.

This is generally the format we would recommend:

Prior to Meeting:

Read/re-read the designated chapters. Complete questions in the Study Guide.

Meeting Day:

(There is a great deal of potential regarding what to discuss, so please be sensitive to the needs of the group, through the Holy Spirit's direction. If you feel led to delve into a topic, then stick with it. Otherwise, keep an eye on the clock, and try to keep the discussion for each chapter to 15 minutes each.)

Open with prayer.

Using a rough guideline of four to six minutes per question, choose several questions to focus on. Where Scripture readings are indicated, consider asking different group members to read these passages aloud before discussing them.

Using this time frame, you should be able to cover four chapters of *Fire & Flood* in an hour's meeting (and you can adjust this according to the amount of time you have for your group).

Close in prayer. Let everyone know which chapters you will be covering in your next meeting.

"We don't know what is before us, but if we have received Jesus Christ, let storms come, let deaths come, let sickness come, let pestilence come; we are sure of life beyond the grave."
D.L. Moody

Preface

God certainly works in amazing and mysterious ways, doesn't He?

At the beginning of the COVID-19 pandemic, I had been teaching a women's Bible study on prayer, using a popular women's devotional book as a guide. To put it plainly, I was a little disappointed with the lack of Scripture found within its pages and had to supplement some of the content. When making plans for our future study, the other leaders and I met to discuss potential devotionals or classes. It was then that one of my dear friends, Cathy Hodges, mentioned that her friend, Dawn Morris, was teaching a class on Revelation. I was intrigued and decided to sign up.

Other than an introductory course taken back in my Bible school days, I hadn't had much instruction on this strange, final chapter of the Bible. Back in my childhood, I had heard friends recount parts of the movie, *A Thief in the Night*, by Jim Grant, accompanied by its haunting theme song "I Wish We'd All Been Ready" by Larry Norman. I remember having nightmares about being "left behind" and, truth be told, I wanted nothing to do with the End Times or End Times theology. At the time, I felt it was enough to know Jesus personally and to know that one day, He would return. *Probably not in my lifetime, though,* I always thought to myself. I figured I could focus on just about everything else in the Bible.

However, because I wanted a study that was biblically sound and full of Scripture, and was struggling to find what I was looking for, I decided to give Dawn's class a try. Besides, I was curious about all those horsemen and monsters and other...things.

At her class, Dawn passionately laid out the differences between Christian eschatology, or interpretations of Revelation, and why these differences are important: we are living in the End Times! I asked a lot of questions, which she graciously answered. Friends, I mean it when I say she gave me hope when the days were dark (remember, this is in the middle of the pandemic and times felt very uncertain), focusing on evidence of God's Great Plan. It amazed me to think that God would be so organized and thoughtfully in control of what was happening to His children and His creation. Dawn explained how God even set up history with examples of what He was going to do through Jesus Christ…giving us great hope and peace in such a crazy time. Could it be true? Could I dare to hope that He could be that good?

At the time, Dawn had just finished writing her book *Fire & Flood,* and invited me to read an early preview. I then wrote a review on her Facebook page, which somehow caught the eye of Christine Gilge, who leads and runs Adorned in Grace in Tacoma—an organization that fights human trafficking. Christine called me to ask if I would be open to participating in the creation of a book study for Dawn's novel. After lots of prayer and discussion, we agreed that I would begin writing in whatever way the Holy Spirit led.

Creating a study for Dawn's book—with 48 chapters—might seem like a daunting task, but I was excited to realize that that all the trials, tears, joys, studies, and experiences the Lord had walked me through in my life had provided me with insight into some of the issues Dawn brings up in her book.

It is interesting to note that at just this time, in God's perfect timing, it no longer remained possible for me to continue teaching algebra, which I had been teaching two and a half days a week. I was able to focus much of my attention to this study guide, which was completed in record time! Christine and a group of wise women—Lisa Deguzman, Darlene Texeira, and Gloria Stepp—helped me ensure that the Bible verses were correct and helpful; it was my biggest concern and focus that this guide would be theologically accurate. Iron sharpens iron! It was and is essential that other eyes were on this book, testing and praying about the contents. As a group, our goal was that it would glorify God and lead others to Christ's free offer of salvation.

As you, the reader, begin this guide, one thing you must know is that not one single person on this team wants you to take anything at our word alone. Rather, test it against the Bible and read for yourself what God says about it all. We believe that God has used Dawn to point you towards God's Word, to His truth in the Bible, which is so full of wisdom. It is our great hope that you will sort out for yourself what is fact and what is fiction.

To whoever is ready to use and read this study guide, may you know this: beyond a shadow of a doubt, you are loved. So many people have prayed for you—that you will seek God's truth and personally experience His love for you. Jesus covered your sins by His death on an ugly, painful cross two thousand years ago so that you may have salvation. He has provided a tool kit in the Bible for the tough things that life brings you as you walk on this earth. He gives us the blessed assurance that those who believe in Him will have an eternity in Heaven, which will be more fun and lovely than our minds can even imagine! May you dig deep into the Bible as never before and be reassured of His love and amazed by His plan! God is good! Be prepared to be amazed.

Lynnette Field

Chapter 1
Recognizing Deception

I. Looking at the Book

Chapter 1 of *Fire & Flood* opens with a bang! What is the setting (time/place)?

We see a reference to "The Vanishing" on page 1. Describe what you know about this reference.

Describe Dani's mother, Karen. Why would her own mother hate Dani with such vehemence?

Describe Jack (the person Dani thought was her father). Is the family depicted here a plausible one? What evidence do you see today that family health is deteriorating? What are the implications of this for our society? Is it extreme/unusual to think someone could be forced to "marry" someone? Dani was facing a forced marriage to Dominic, the cult leader. It was a horrible thought to begin with, but the twisted "yuck" increased when we realized their actual relationship was as . . . ?!! Do you believe things like this happen in the world today?

Describe Daphne. What examples do we have in today's world of people being killed for standing up for someone else?

II. Looking at the Bible

Many people think they will be able to recognize the wolf in sheep's clothing, but Jesus wouldn't have warned us about them if they weren't truly hard to recognize! God gives us a strong warning about altering anything He says:

> "But even if we, or an angel from heaven, should preach to you a gospel contrary to what we have preached to you, he is to be accursed. As we have said before, so I say again now, if any man is preaching to you a gospel contrary to what you received, he is to be accursed!" (Galatians 1:8-9)

In the space below, list some characteristics of a false prophet/teacher. Look up Matthew 7:15-19 and 2 Corinthians 11:13-15.

How do they appear?

What kind of authority do they claim?

What gives away their true nature?

Compare 2 Peter 1, which describes a true teacher, with false teachers in 2 Peter 2:

	True Teachers: 2 Peter 1	False Teachers: 2 Peter 2
Source: What or who is the source of their message?	vv.1, 12–21	v.1
Method: What is the substance of their message?		
Results: In what position will their message leave you?		vv.1–3, 17–22
Character Traits: What kind of people does their message produce?		
Fruits: What result does the message have in people's lives?		
Eternal Consequence: Where does the message ultimately leave you?		

Jesus warned His disciples, "Not everyone who says to Me, 'Lord, Lord,' will enter the kingdom of heaven, but he who does the will of My Father who is in heaven will enter" (Matthew 7:21).

Now go back to 2 Peter 3:17-18, which sums it all up! What do you observe?

"Be on your _____, so that _____, but _____."

III. Looking at Ourselves:

Do you have a Daphne in your life—someone who loves you unconditionally? How do they demonstrate their love for you?

How do you recognize the signs that someone is in a cult? Does it always involve people isolating themselves from the rest of society?

How would you get help for a situation like this?

Chapter 2
Evildoers

I. Looking at the Book:

Briefly describe the Nephilim as author Dawn Morris has described them in this chapter.

Describe the Magistrate (in character as well as appearance).

Why would this environment focus so intently on sensuality?

Note on page 10: "Only those sympathetic to the Old Ways found anything wrong with expressions of strong desires." Why would there be anything wrong with strong desires?

Sum up the Magistrate and Nephilim in one word:

Page 11: "Any questioning of the ruling power against immoral behavior…"
Why wouldn't the Magistrate or his government welcome discussion?

Compare this to what is currently going on in our own culture with censorship by Big Tech platforms and others. How does this line up with the U.S. Constitution and the Bill of Rights (Bill #1 in particular)?

II. Looking at the Bible:

Read Genesis 6:1-2, 4. What does it say about the "Nephilim"?

Find other Bible references to "Nephilim." Who/what does the Bible (God) say they are?

Check out https://www.gotquestions.org/Nephilim.html
Mark 5:15 says that demons (fallen angels) can do what?

III. Looking at Ourselves:
Why would fear also be enticing?

Do you find that beauty and evil attract you? How?

How could great intelligence manipulate and deceive, and why would it?

How can revulsion pair with longing?

Knowing that these situations may not be healthy, how can we protect ourselves from succumbing?

Chapter 3

The Rapture

I. Looking at the Book:

What are some physical differences in the landscape described in Chapter 3 (after "The Vanishing") compared to how things are now (e.g., lakes, mountains, sunshine, trees)?

Is it possible that someone or something woke Dani to protect her during the earthquake? What evidence could you give to suggest that she was being protected?

What themes run through this chapter regarding knowledge?

What themes run throughout this chapter regarding women?

What themes run throughout this chapter regarding control?

What foreshadowing occurs?

II. Looking at the Bible:

What does Isaiah 49:15 say about God as our Father compared to human parents?

Sometimes, God sends the protection of angels! What does the angel of the Lord do? (See Psalm 34:7.)

How does God use angels to help us? (See Daniel 6:22, 10:12-14.)

Whom do angels help? (See Hebrews 1:14.)

Revelation 6 states that God's wrath will be poured out onto the earth during the Tribulation. What verses suggest that the landscape will look like the world as Dani sees it in Chapter 3?

III. Looking at Ourselves:

Knowledge is power. Is this true? Why or why not?

Bad things happen . . . but could there be a reason for them? What are your personal thoughts on the idea that "bad things happen for a reason?"

Have there been any times that you have felt God's presence? What about a lack of His presence?

Chapter 4
Old Ways

I. Looking at the Book:

Sometimes we think people in the Ancient World (or Old Testament) lived in tents or caves.

What examples of conveniences and refinement do you find evidence of in this chapter?

What exactly does it mean when the author mentions "The Old Ways"?

Does it surprise you that Methuselah is in this chapter, along with Noah? What evidence do we have in the Bible that points towards this truth?

Check out: https://answersingenesis.org/bible-timeline/genealogy/when-did-methuselah-die/

II. Looking at the Bible:

Let's take a look at some Bible references that give a picture of a healthy family life.

Read Genesis 2:24. How does God want a husband and wife to relate to one another?

Next, read Psalm 133. What should be the goal of family members?

What is this compared with?

Read Ephesians 6:1-4. What is the promise for children who keep this commandment?

What warning and command does God give to fathers here?

III. Looking at Ourselves:

The Bible gives families instructions for doing life together—it's the "Old Way."

How might you have moved away from the "Old Ways," with reference to biblical values and our own culture today? If you have, what steps or attitude changes could you take to move toward what God originally intended?

Chapter 5
End Times, Part 1

I. Looking at the Book:

Briefly explain how countries are being governed in Dani's reality.

Who are the Global Union Soldiers, and what role do they play? Who is at conflict with the GUS? (e.g., fringe groups?)

What are the characteristics of Christians and "Old Christianity" that Tomas details to Dani?

Are these true?

Is there a positive aspect to these characteristics?

Why can a twisted truth be more believable than an outright deception?

II. Looking at the Bible:

Read the Scripture passage quoted in Chapter 5, Psalm 18:16-17. Whom does David credit for saving him from his enemies?

Read Revelation 11:3-12. Who are the Witnesses? Who is their Lord (v.8)?

What testimony would they be giving to the world for the first three and a half years under the wrath of God?

In John 14:6, Jesus says, "I am the Way, the Truth, and the Light. NO ONE comes to the Father except through Me." What does that mean?

Can this truth be altered?

In the Old Testament, believers looked forward to the Messiah and His salvation. In what many scholars believe to be the oldest book in the Bible, Job stated boldly that he knew his Redeemer lived, that he (Job) would one day stand on the earth, and that in his flesh he would see the Lord (see Job 19:23-27). Similarly, in the New Testament, the apostle Paul clearly laid out the fact that salvation is and always has been a matter of faith.

Look at Romans 10:5-11. According to this passage, what do you have to do to become a child of God?

III. Looking at Ourselves:

Is it possible to be loving and take a strong stance on truth in our culture?

If you were to die tonight, do you have confidence that you'd be in Heaven?

If you did die and God were to ask you why He should let you into Heaven, what would be your answer?

How can you share this gospel message with others in a loving way that is solid on truth and your convictions?

"It is bad enough to be without money, or without health, or without home or without friends, but it's far worse to be without Christ."
J.C. Ryle

Chapter 6

The Problem

I. Looking at the Book:

In the wedding chamber, Ariana experiences overwhelming grief, and doesn't know what to expect. Do you think it is beautiful or sad that Ariana is expected to marry, and doesn't seem to be hesitant about the situation in which she finds herself?

Why does the Magistrate tempt Ariana with a vision of children, laughter, loving looks, and longing?

Why might these things be hollow in this situation?

What does Jesus tell us about marriage?

> *"God . . . is not opposed to our enjoyment of sex within marriage. He designed it and gave it to Adam and Eve. Satan tries to malign the goodness of God by making us think that God is trying to take our fun away by restricting sex to marriage. But God knows that it creates major problems when we violate His design for His gift. We need to regard marriage and sex in marriage as God's good gift, designed for our pleasure, to meet our deepest needs for human companionship. In the context of marriage, we can thankfully enjoy what God has given."*
>
> **Steven J. Cole, Sermon,**
> **"God's Design for Marriage"**

II. Looking at the Bible:

How did God communicate with His people in the Old Testament? Why couldn't everyone in the Old Testament speak directly to God?

In this chapter, Jesus appears to Ariana. While God can speak to us supernaturally, it's His written Word that we are to follow: "Faith comes by hearing, and hearing by the word of God" (Romans 10:17).

The Word of God is the means God has given us to defend ourselves from the enemy of our souls. Jesus used Scripture every time Satan tempted Him. Look up Hebrews 4:12. How is this heavenly weapon described?

When the enemy appeared to Ariana, he tempted her with lies and partial truths. How does Satan tempt and lure us away from God and anything good?

Starting in the Garden of Eden, we see Satan's hatred for mankind. Those who follow Jesus Christ are the enemies of Satan and the fallen angels who follow him. Read Paul's warning to the church of Ephesus in Acts 20:28-31.

Why did Paul command them to be alert? What danger were they in?

Why is it that some people don't see the difference between darkness and light? Read 2 Corinthians 4:2-5.

Jesus taught truth in parables. Here He's speaking not only to the disciples around Him, but to a future generation that sees the signs of the end. What does He tell us to do? (See Luke 21:29-36.)

III. Looking at Ourselves:

How do feelings of shame and unworthiness battle with God's desire for us to be confident of His love and without fear? Are we ever alone?

How can we know that God does love us and wants us to be courageous when we don't see a physical presence of God standing in front of us, or hear His voice out loud?

How does Satan tempt you?

Chapter 7
Sealed

I. Looking at the Book:

In this chapter, we meet Mitch and Sierra. Where are they geographically? How did they come to be on the scene?

Dani doesn't understand what it means to love Jesus and trust in Him, but she is "sealed"! What protection does that provide for her, both seen and unseen?

II. Looking at the Bible:

Read Revelation 9 and take note of the horse/locust/man, whose sting is like a scorpion.

What does it mean to be "sealed"? (See Ephesians 1:13-14.)

How can you know for sure that you are sealed?

Read 2 Corinthians 1:21-22. Can one ever lose the seal of God?

III. Looking at Ourselves:

Have you ever been stung by a scorpion, or some other insect? How did it feel?

What would you do to prevent that from happening again?

What would you do to protect someone you loved from the pain of a sting that lasted five months?

Physically?

Spiritually?

Chapter 8
God Loves Animals

I. Looking at the Book:

In this chapter, we see the unique perspective of Noah's project from someone who isn't Noah. In the days before the wedding, how does the family interact and relate with each other?

How are responsibilities divided?

II. Looking at the Bible

Why did God tell Noah to build the Ark? (See Genesis 6: 9-22.)

Was the Ark available, pre-Flood, to all who believed in God?

Of course, the Creator is not like us, but we can learn a great deal about Him by analyzing what the Bible says. What does the detailed description God gave to Noah tell you about Him?

What does God's salvation for the animals reveal about Him?

Do we have any clues that there will be animals on the New Earth? (See Isaiah 11:6-9, 65:25; Revelation 5:13.)

III. Looking at Ourselves:

God loves all His creation; He created animals and placed them in the Garden of Eden. Even though our ancestors lost Eden, mankind still enjoys the wonder of this part of God's creation because He rescued the animals on the Ark.

One of the most detailed periods of time described in the Bible is the Millennial Reign of Jesus Christ. Read Isaiah 11:6-9 and discuss how the animal world will be different when the King of Kings is reigning over our world.

From Revelation 19:11-14, we know there are animals in Heaven. What do you think it will be like to ride a heavenly horse?

Here's a link to what Randy Alcorn, the author of *Heaven,* has to say about God's love for animals:
https://www.epm.org/static/uploads/downloads/12_Chapter_39.pdf

Chapter 9
Coincidences

I. Looking at the Book:
What are the coincidences to which Mitch is referring?

What are "the really bad judgments"?

II. Looking at the Bible:
God is in control, so is there really such a thing as coincidence?

Look up and take note of what you find:
Proverbs 19:21, 16:33

Isaiah 46: 9-11

Romans 8:28

III. Looking at Ourselves

What do you think "seals" you for God? Reading the Bible? Is it being a good person? Something else?

Look up Ephesians 1:13 to see what God says about this issue and record your observations here.

What does a world facing God's wrath look like? Why is that not what He wants for you?

"God's plan is to save believers from their sins—and to bring them fully and finally to Himself (John 3:16-18; 2 Timothy 2:10; 2 Peter 3:9). Believers have been saved from the penalty of their sins; they are currently being saved from the power of sin. One day, when God's plan of salvation is completed and they are with Christ, they will be like Him, and they will be saved even from the very presence of sin. This is God's plan of salvation. God's ultimate purpose in redemptive history is to create a people, from every tribe and nation, to dwell in His presence, glorifying Him through their lives and enjoying Him forever." [1]

---

1   "God's Overall Plan." The Elegant Farmer. Accessed July 25, 2022. http://www. elegantfarmer.com/wp-content/uploads/2014/08/GODS-OVERALL-PLAN.pdf.

Chapter 10
Conflicts

I. Looking at the Book:

In this chapter, we meet more characters and read about the dynamic between them. What does a healthy relationship between Japheth, Ariana, Noah, Laelah, Shem, and Nua look like?

What is it about Ham in particular that gives us pause as to his character?

II. Looking at the Bible:

Does God use situations we might think are unfortunate to protect His beloved children? Read through Romans 8:28 to help you frame your answer.

III. Looking at Ourselves:

Go back to page 68 in *Fire & Flood*. Noah didn't run and hide, but rather he confronted situations and dealt with them head on. What can we learn from this? How can we apply this concept to our own lives?

Humiliation, shame, or fear of what people might say often stops us from maximizing opportunities in front of us. If you didn't fear what people said, what would you do differently? How would your life be different if you lived without fear of what other people thought?

"If you read history, you will find that the Christians who did most for the present world were just those who thought most of the next."
Randy Alcorn, *Heaven*

Do you know anyone who exemplifies the quote above?

Chapter 11

Tribulation

I. Looking at the Book:

Describe what happens in the Tribulation from what you have read in Chapter 10. Why does it happen?

II. Looking at the Bible:

What is the "Tribulation"?

1. Daniel 9:24: God will finish His discipline over the nation of

    _____.

2. Matthew 24:21: There will be a great tribulation such as the

    _____ has never known.

Why does the Tribulation take place?

We don't have to guess! God has already told us. Look up the following verses that detail the three main purposes for the Tribulation:
1. Isaiah 13:9: To make an end of _____ and _____ people
2. Revelation 7:1-4, 9-14: To bring about a revival from every _____
3. Daniel 12:5-7; Zechariah 12:10: To bring the nation of _____ back into fellowship with Him

III. Looking at Ourselves:
Is it okay to wonder or question beliefs you or others might have about the end times? Why or why not?

Do you wonder why God would allow the Tribulation to happen?

Chapter 12
The Bride of Christ

I. Looking at the Book:

This chapter gives us a glimpse into the romantic life of a married couple. Japheth and Ariana began to "see the joy and pleasure in married life." What examples do you see of how they made this happen?

II. Looking at the Bible:

How does Japheth's care for Ariana resemble God's care for His Bride, the Church?

(Read Ephesians 5: 27; Revelation 19: 7-9, 21: 2.)

III. Looking at Ourselves:

List *practical* ways you can be a more loving spouse, parent, or friend:

- I can put love into action by doing this for: _____
- Mon __ Tues __ Wed __ Thur __ Fri __ Sat __ Sun __ (check and repeat)
- For _____, I can put love into action by doing this: _____
- Mon __ Tues __ Wed __ Thur __ Fri __ Sat __ Sun __ (check and repeat)
- For <line for reader response>, I can put love into action by doing this: _____
- Mon __ Tues __ Wed __ Thur __ Fri __ Sat __ Sun __ (check and repeat)

"Because Satan hates us, he's determined to rob us of the joy we'd have if we believed what God tells us about the magnificent world to come."
Randy Alcorn, *Heaven*

Chapter 13

Martyrs

I. Looking at the Book:

This chapter paints a grisly picture of what they did to people with the guillotine. Why do you think they would have targeted these people?

II. Looking at the Bible

What does the Bible say about martyrs? See the following passages for information and record your observations below:

Matthew 14:1-12

Acts 7:54-60, 12:1-2

Revelation 2:12-13, 6:9-11, 11:7-8, 20:4

III. Looking at Ourselves:

Why would it not be the worst thing to lose your life for Christ?

Does your heart ever wrestle with your head when you think about this?

Are you willing to cross the line, to say or do *anything*, that would even put you in this position?

Are you willing to declare your love for Jesus out loud, to a public forum, regardless of consequences?

If you believe the Bible to be true, how did Jesus declare His love for YOU?

"Meanwhile, we on this dying Earth can relax and rejoice for our loved ones who are in the presence of Christ. As the apostle Paul tells us, though we naturally grieve at losing loved ones, we are not "to grieve like the rest of men, who have no hope" (1 Thessalonians 4:13). Our parting is not the end of our relationship, only an interruption. We have not "lost" them, because we know where they are. They are experiencing the joy of Christ's presence in a place so wonderful that Christ called it Paradise. And one day, we're told, in a magnificent reunion, they and we "will be with the Lord forever. Therefore **encourage each other with these words**" (1 Thessalonians 4:17-1)."

Randy Alcorn, *Heaven*

Chapter 14

The Ark

I. Looking at the Book:

In this scene, why was Ariana paralyzed with fear? What happened that helped her overcome her fear?

II. Looking at the Bible:

Check out the account of the Ark in the Bible, in Genesis 6: 14-21. Does the author accurately and biblically represent the Ark? How so?

Have you ever thought about the origins of the world in a literal sense?

Check out AnswersinGenesis.org:
https://answersingenesis.org/noahs-ark/fantastic-voyage-how-could-noah-care-animals/
. . . and God's World Exploration Station
https://godsworldexplorationstation.com/

In 2 Timothy 1:7, we read about dealing with fear. In Psalm 143:1-6 (especially in verse 5), we learn again how to confront it. How do you deal with your fear?

III. Looking at Ourselves:

In this chapter, we read this phrase: "Don't look . . . just take action. " In what situations is this applicable/helpful?

How can the Creator be trusted if He is willing to destroy the whole world?

Why would God allow Ham, who has the "look" of the Magistrate, to survive with the others on the Ark?

"Safe?" said Mr. Beaver, *"Who said anything about safe?*
'COURSE He isn't SAFE.
But He's good. HE'S THE KING, I TELL YOU."
C.S. Lewis, *The Lion, the Witch, and the Wardrobe*

Chapter 15

Betrayal

I. Looking at the Book:

Have you ever crossed a land border into another country (for example, the border from the U.S. into Canada and/or vice versa)? Imagine what would have to happen if our border crossings were abandoned. Describe the troubling border situations today.

In this chapter, Dani is betrayed (yet again) by Mitch, a father figure to her. Why did Mitch submit to receiving the mark? Can love ever justify such betrayal? Whom did Mitch actually betray?

II. Looking at the Bible:

What is the mark of the beast in Revelation? Read Revelation 13:15-18.

What is required to get it?

Some people worry that they will "accidently" get the mark, through a chip or mark inserted without their knowledge. Do you think this is a legitimate concern?

III. Looking at Ourselves:

Is there anything you love so much that would be worth betrayal? Why or why not?

Chapter 16

Work

I. Looking at the Book:

Feeding the animals is a lot of work on the Ark! Imagine being around animals that now might elicit fear in you (e.g., lions, tigers, bears) and caring for them! What animals would you be afraid of, and what animals would you gravitate towards, if any?

II. Looking at the Bible:

What does God say about work? Will we work in Heaven, and why will it not feel like the laborious, boring, unwelcome work we experience here on Earth?

Will there be animals in Heaven?

Check out the following commentary and verses, and read about this for yourself: [2]

> *"Thinking that heaven will be boring betrays a heresy—that God is boring. Nonsense! God made our taste buds, adrenaline, the nerve endings that convey pleasure to our brains, our imaginations, and our capacity for happiness and excitement: "No longer will there be any curse. The throne of God and of the Lamb will be in the city, and his servants will serve him."*
> **Revelation 22:3, NIV**

> *"Servants have things to do, places to go, people to see. Our most common everyday activities will be worship, punctuated by the joy of joining the multitudes to praise him. Jesus spoke of the 'renewal of all things.'"*
> **Matthew 19:28, NIV**

---

2   Alcorn, Randy. "Let Go of Lies about Heaven: 8 Myths Many Believe." Desiring God. June 5, 2020. https://www.desiringgod.org/articles/let-go-of-lies-about-heaven.

"Peter preached that Christ will remain in heaven 'until the time for restoring all the things about which God spoke by the mouth of his holy prophets.'"
Acts 3:21

"Yet somehow, we've overlooked an entire biblical vocabulary. Reconcile. Redeem. Restore. Recover. Return. Renew. Resurrect. God plans to physically restore his entire creation, including us, earth, and animals."[3]
Isaiah 11:6–9, 65:17, 25; Romans 8:19–23

III. Looking at Ourselves:

Do you find that it is better to be busy than to have the time to sit and be anxious? Or do you enjoy quiet/solitude?

---

3   Piper, John. *Desiring God.* Multnomah Books, 1996.

Chapter 17
End Times, Part 2

I.   Looking at the Book:

We learned a lot about allegiance to evil in this chapter. Does allegiance to evil bring about safety? Explain.

What kind of mother hates her child? What kind of father would kill his baby?

II. Looking at the Bible:

What does Jesus predict about the end times in the chapter of Matthew 24?

What He Says WILL Happen

What He Says HE Will Do

What He Says WE Should Do

What does God want for His people? How do we know?

III. Looking at Ourselves:

Evil can be dressed like healthy, happy, and protected people. It can be deceiving. How can you discern the difference between good and evil, when on the surface things might look to be just fine (or even better than the alternative)?

Are there any other novels that depict evil as deceptively beautiful at first? If you are familiar with *The Lion, the Witch, and the Wardrobe*, by C.S. Lewis, how do you see this idea in that story?

"A wolf is a predator, and an expert at deceit. 'Wolves' are able to look like sheep and talk like sheep. They are NOT obvious. Outwardly, they look harmless and are kind with good intentions but inwardly, they are full of hate and evil. They teach false doctrine and can even disguise it amongst sound truth.
They make it attractive."
@mrsjgarwood on IG

Chapter 18

Isolation

I. Looking at the Book:

A hundred days in isolation? Wow! Thanks to COVID-19 and its associated lockdowns, we now know a bit about what that would feel like. What did you do to pass the time during the COVID lockdowns? What things did Noah and his family do to pass the time?

II. Looking at the Bible:

Read Genesis 8:1-8. What does "remembered" mean to you, compared to what it means to God? It is not merely "to recall to mind." It is also to express concern for someone, and to act with loving care for him or her.

Also read Nehemiah 5:19 and 13:31.

III. Looking at Ourselves:

Change! How does it affect you? Is it difficult for you to accept change, or do you embrace it?

How has change been a positive thing in your life? Have you ever thought that in hindsight, you shouldn't have worried about it?

After the flood, the topography of the world changed, as Ariana experienced. Imagine a world where *you* don't know where anything is.

The Bible tells us that someday, we will live in a new Heaven and a new Earth (see Revelation 21). When you think of living in a new reality, just as the family in the Ark experienced, does it make you excited?

*"We should **daily** look forward to a world without evil, suffering, or death, where God will live with us and wipe away our tears forever (Revelation 21:4). Anticipating the glorious realities of the resurrected earth has breathtaking implications for our present happiness and our sense of the far-reaching scope of the gospel message."*
John Piper, *Desiring God*

Chapter 19
True Believers

I.   Looking at the Book:

Trace Dani's journeys on the map in the Appendix.

Who is the "true believer" in this chapter? Is this an accurate representation of a true believer?

What is the difference between someone who seeks truth and the people characterized as "true believers" in this chapter?

How did God come to rescue Dani through adversity in this chapter?

II. Looking at the Bible:

Did you notice how biblical attributes or terms are distorted by the people in this chapter? There is a difference between the true Christianity and counterfeit religions. While Christianity does include rules and rituals, those things are not what makes a follower of Jesus right before God. Other religions say "Do," while Christianity says, "Done."

Our good deeds don't make us Christians; accepting the truths in the verses below is what makes us Christians:

Romans 10:9-10

Ephesians 1:7

John 1:12

Read Matthew 7:15. Describe how the Bible uses the analogy of wolves in sheep's clothing.

Discuss how people are deceived by counterfeit religion.

III. Looking at Ourselves:

What does true salvation look like, and how is it different from what "the world" proclaims as salvation?

How does one become saved? (If you are considering this question, please jump ahead to Chapter 25.)

What are some ways we can look for wolves in sheep's clothing in our world today? The wisdom of the Bible is clear; it is not easy to discern the wolves, especially when they look exactly like sheep. It will not be obvious, or God would not have to warn us! How can we stay sharp?

"A false gospel imagines that God's kingdom is of this world, and that believers are called to transform this world. The true gospel teaches that this world is our enemy, has nothing to offer us and is under Satan's influence."
Rick Becker

Chapter 20
Population Realities

I.   Looking at the Book:

How did the author suggest Earth was repopulated after the flood?

What was the first thing Noah and his family did when they got off the Ark? Why would that be important?

It's interesting to note that Laelah was careful to protect seeds and grow plants. How was this repopulation growth similar and different to what occurred after the Garden of Eden and the Fall?

II. Looking at the Bible:

Read about the account of Noah's indiscretion in Genesis 9:20-25.

The Bible is the only religious book that shares the sins of its saints. Why do you think God included this in biblical accounts?

Read Psalm 127:3-5; Matthew 19:13-14; Romans 13:7; 1 Timothy 5:1.

What does God say are the consequences of disrespect and a poor attitude?

III. Looking at Ourselves:

Have you ever planted a garden? Did you know that there are International Seed Banks? Look up https://time.com/doomsday-vault/. What are your thoughts about this?

How does today's culture regard the "blessing" of having babies? How does this differ from what God says in Psalm 127?

Would this (should this) affect our attitudes toward pregnancy planning, and our lives in general, in these current times? This can be a challenging teaching moment in our busy, controlled, modern lives. We must look at the Bible to seek His truth, in everything, and be willing to trust God, even with this matter.

Chapter 21

Decision Making

I. Looking at the Book:

In this chapter, we take a look at trust, which is a reoccurring theme. Dani (dryly) stated, "Trusting men who were offering help has not gone well for me up to this point." (See *Fire & Flood*, page 130.) Why do you think she trusted Jannik?

Were there any signs that she shouldn't relax and trust him?

II. Looking at the Bible:

What is the sign of the Anti-Christ? Read Revelation 13:1-18 and Revelation 19:20.

While the Bible gives many titles to the coming evil world leader, we know him by the title "Anti-Christ."

Read 2 Thessalonians 2:1-10. What is Paul talking about?

What is keeping the Anti-Christ from coming onto the world scene?

Is the Anti-Christ going to be allowed to continue ruling this world?

Who will bring him to an end?

For further reading, the following verses also provide information on the Anti-Christ:
Matthew 24:5,24

Mark 13:6, 22

2 Thessalonians 2:3-12

1 John 2:18-22, 4: 1-3

2 John 1:7

III. Looking at Ourselves:
What are some healthy strategies for decision making?

Here is one method for making decisions with a Christian worldview:[4]

1. What biblical principles should inform my decision? (See Proverbs 2:6.)

2. Do I have ALL the facts—pros and cons?

3. Is the pressure of time forcing me to make a premature decision? (See Proverbs 19:2.)

4. What are the possible motives driving my decision? (See Proverbs 16:2.)

5. How should past experiences inform me?

4 "Should I? Decision-Making Principles. Accessed July 25, 2022. https://assets.ctfassets. net/hw5pse7y1ojx/3cjegWmbJQ7WXv5icMCGvm/d4aa7f8fec1f50eae328f1a33e5884f5/ Should_I_2019.pdf

6. What is the collective counsel of my community? (See Proverbs 11:14.)

7. Have I honestly considered the warning signs? (See Proverbs 10:17.)

8. Have I considered the possible outcomes for my course of action? (See Proverbs 14:1.)

9. Could this decision jeopardize my integrity or hinder my witness for the Lord? (See Proverbs 25:26.)

10. Is there a better option that would allow me to make a greater impact for God's Kingdom? (See Proverbs 11:30.)

Chapter 22
Languages

I.   Looking at the Book:

Have you ever visited a part of the world where you haven't been able to understand the language? What was that like?

What is the beauty of sharing a language?

What are the challenges when you don't, and how are they overcome?

II.   Looking at the Bible:

Noah's father was alive during Adam's time! Isn't that fascinating? What evidence do we have that this is true? (See the Appendix for a chart that shows the overlap of the lifespans of early figures in the Bible.)

How might the presence of the Nephilim on the earth at that time help to explain why God would say He regretted making men and women?

What are the characteristics and qualities of God, as described in the Bible, that show He is incompatible with evil, and that He is just, loving, and merciful?

Psalm 145:9: "The Lord is _____ to all, and His tender mercies are over _____ His works."

1 Samuel 2:2: "There is no one _____ like the Lord, indeed, there is no one besides You, nor is there any rock like our God."

While God is ALL of those things, He is at the same time, a righteous God who is just.

Exodus 34:6-7: "The Lord is passionate and _____, slow to _____, and abounding in lovingkindness and _____: who keeps

_____, who forgives _____, transgression and sin; yet He will by no means leave the _____ unpunished."

> *"God's wrath in the Bible is never the capricious, self-indulgent, irritable, morally ignoble thing that human anger so often is. It is, instead, a right and necessary reaction to objective moral evil."*
> **J.I. Packer,** *Knowing God*

III. Looking at Ourselves:

Distance, whether emotional or physical, can cause families to drift apart (see *Fire & Flood*, page 147). Is this a natural eventuality, or should we fight for community and unity within our families?

What are some ways to do this?

> *"'As the heavens are higher than the earth, so are my ways higher than your ways and my thoughts than your thoughts.' God's thoughts are indeed higher than ours, but when he reduces his thoughts into words and reveals them in Scripture, he expects us to study them, meditate on them, and understand them—again, not exhaustively, but accurately."*
> **Randy Alcorn,** *Heaven*

Chapter 23

The Beast and the Witnesses

I.   Looking at the Book:

In what way does Bellomo make himself like Jesus Christ in the same city where He died?

Whom do people think he is?

In what strategic way do Cain and Bellomo set up the meeting with the Witnesses?

II. Looking at the Bible:

What does Revelation 13:3-6 tell you about "the beast"?

Why do you think people would follow without question?

Read Revelation 11:7-13. What happens to the Witnesses?

How does the Bible describe this scene?

Bible skeptics in years past used to cite this passage to "prove" the Bible isn't true, saying, "There's no way the entire world will see their dead bodies for three and a half days." Now that we can watch whatever we want—from all over the world—on our smart phones or other devices, this argument no longer holds any water!

III. Looking at Ourselves:

Your view about Israel matters. Long ago, God promised Abraham He would bless those who bless Israel and curse those who curse Israel (see Genesis 12:3). This covenant still stands!

Dr. David Jeremiah, in his book, *The Book of Signs*, states, ". . . leaders and nations that ally with Israel to preserve, protect, and defend it will likewise be preserved, protected, and defended. On the other hand, those who stand in the way of Israel's well-being will find themselves standing against God—which means they will not long stand at all."[5] In Zechariah 2:8, the prophet Zechariah declared that God would plunder the nations that plunder Israel.

According to Zechariah, why is this so?

With this in mind, it seems clear we must do all we can to bless Israel, simply because God tells us He wishes us to do so!

---

5   Jeremiah, Dr. David. *Book of Signs: 31 Undeniable Prophecies of the Apocalypse.* Thomas Nelson Publishing, 2020, p. 9.

There's a belief going around that says God's covenants with Israel have been transferred to the Church, even though Paul wrote three chapters in his letter to the Roman church about the fact that God's not done with Israel. (See Romans 9-11.)

> *"I say then, God has not rejected His people, has He? Far from it! For I too am an Israelite, a descendant of Abraham, of the tribe of Benjamin. God has not rejected His people whom He foreknew."*
> **Romans 11:1-2a**

How does this passage confirm or challenge your thoughts about God's heart for the Jewish people?

The Church is separate from the Jewish people, as the true believers who make up the Church are the Bride of Christ (who will be raptured), whereas Jews are God's Chosen People. Because the Jews as a nation do not believe in Christ (Jesus made it very clear that NO ONE comes to the Father but through Him), they will be present during the Tribulation, but then will come to an awareness, *as a nation,* that Jesus is Lord of all, and therefore will then be saved and restored because of their covenant with God.

Next, let's talk about miracles, since that topic also comes up in this chapter. Why would it be important to distinguish between wanting a miracle for your own advantage, as compared to wanting to honor God no matter the outcome?

Consider the quote from Charles Spurgeon below; does this influence how you answer the above question? What do you think Spurgeon meant by this quote?

"Dear Friends,
If you begin to seek signs, and if you were to see them,
do you know what would happen? Why, you would
want more: and when you had these, you would
demand still more. It is ingrained in human nature thus
to see a sign: but what is that but idolatry?"
C.H. Spurgeon

Chapter 24
Power

I. Looking at the Book:

Theatre vs. Life: How does Nimrod stage his palace and the throne room to create a psychological atmosphere of power?

Why does Ariana feel like she lacks charm and youthfulness for the first time in her life? (See *Fire & Flood*, page 160.)

Who are the three men who approach Shem and Japheth's group in the field?

What is the significance of the blessing?

II. Looking at the Bible:

How does God say we should see ourselves, without theatrics and with complete honesty?

We stand _____ before God, the _____ Judge (Romans 5:12,18).

We are _____ by sin (John 8:34).

We are not able to do _____ because of our _____ (Romans 7:18).

We are dying physically and dead _____ (Ephesians 2:1-10), but God, even when we were _____ in our transgressions, made us _____ together with Christ; by grace you have been saved.

> "Fortunately for us, God loves His enemies, and He demonstrated His great love for us by sending His only begotten Son to die in our place (John 3:16–21; Romans 5:8). We were lost, and the Good Shepherd gathered His sheep; we were spiritually blind, and the Healer found us; we stood guilty before God, and the Judge has justified us; we were enslaved, and the Redeemer has paid the price for our release; we were morally ruined, and He has restored us; we were dead, and the Resurrection and the Life has raised us up."[6]

III. Looking at Ourselves:

Do you live your life confident and content in the way God views you? Is your focus inward or outward (upward)? Why or why not—what is stopping you?

---

6   "What Is the Human Condition, According to the Bible?" Got Questions. Accessed July 25, 2022. https://www.gotquestions.org/human-condition.html

Chapter 25
The Power of Salvation

I. Looking at the Book:
Why are the men and women separated when they enter King David's Tomb?

Would you share Dani's irritation?

What is the difference between people in this story who don't have Christ in their lives, and have hardened their hearts, and the people who have faith in Jesus?

How does Tamas ask Dani to believe in Jesus?

What kind of faith does it take to pack up and move without taking anything with you, with no time to warn anyone you love?

II. Looking at the Bible:

Now...for the most important part of this novel, this guide, and the most important part for YOU!!! This part is SO important we have printed these verses out for you, but be sure to look them up and find these verses for yourself within the Bible.

> *"For all have sinned and fall short of the glory of God."*
> **Romans 3:23**

This is not good news, because sin separates us from God. It's like this: I give you a nice, cold bottle of water that has a tiny bit of toilet water in it. Would you drink that? No, of course not! In the same way, we can't expect holy God to ignore our sin. Even if you have only done one thing wrong in your life, that would separate you from standing in God's holy presence.

It is not enough just to live a good life and be a nice person. Remember, God is EVERYTHING that is pure, good, fun, creative, kind, wise, interesting, intelligent, beautiful, true, worthy, integral, joyful, safe, and healthy.

Heaven is where God is, so to not be with God is to choose to not be in Heaven, either. If being with God equates to all these amazing things, what would the opposite of that be like? Sort of sounds like hell, right? God does talk about hell in the Scriptures, as well as the consequences for sin, and frankly, they aren't good. (See Matthew 25: 46; 2 Thessalonians 1: 6-9; Revelation 21: 8.) But wait! There is good—actually, fantastic—news! Read John 3: 16-17:"For God so loved the world, that He gave His only begotten Son, that whoever believes in Him shall not perish but have eternal life. For God did not send the Son into the world to judge the world, but that the world might be saved through Him." So . . . Jesus can save *you*!!!

Then read John 14: 6-7: "Jesus said to him, '*I am the way, the truth, and the life*; NO ONE comes to the Father but through Me'" (emphasis added). This is the good news; you just have to receive it for yourself: " Yet to all who did receive him, to those who believed in his name, he gave the right to become children of God . . ." (John 1:12).

III. Looking at Ourselves:

Some people think there are a lot of nice-sounding religions out there, and that it would be acceptable to God if one would choose to walk a different path than what we are describing here. Whatever works, right?

But when you think about it, it wouldn't really make sense for the King of Kings to offer Himself up on the cross to die if there was any other way to atone for our sins, would it? Jesus is the only way to have a saving relationship with the Father. God sent Jesus, who was God—completely without sin—to be your sin, so that you might be pure and blameless before God.

You might be thinking, *I want to be saved! How do I do that?* Romans 10: 9 says:

"If you confess with your mouth Jesus is Lord, and believe in your heart that God raised Him from the dead, YOU WILL BE SAVED; for with the heart a person believes, resulting in righteousness, and with the mouth he confesses, resulting in salvation" (emphasis added).

And, Romans 10: 13 tells us: "For whoever calls on the name of the Lord will be saved."

And that's it! It's that simple.

If you believe that Jesus, being God's Son, has fully paid the penalty for your sin, YOU ARE SAVED!!! You are born again into new life with Christ; you are sealed with His Holy Spirit. What a gift!

If you haven't yet believed that Jesus died and rose again to pay the penalty of your sins to save you, would you consider that now? Do you understand that your sin separates you from God, and therefore you will be separated from God's love and the fellowship of His family for all eternity?

But, if you trust that what Jesus did on the cross, the blood He shed, the terrible pain He endured, the pain of suffering the guilt and shame for our wrongdoings, the agonizing separation from the Father He endured, and the debt he paid that *you* owe—you will be saved. Salvation is you simply accepting what Jesus Christ did for you. There is no way anyone can earn or deserve this life-changing gift.

To learn more about your new life as a Christian, God has already provided an amazing guidebook written for you. Read the Bible; it's the TOOL BOOK of life, with lessons from the past, tried and true recipes for living life right now, and detailing plans for the future. It's all there!

We would suggest you start reading the Gospel of John in the New Testament—it's about Jesus' life and provides the essential nuggets of how we should live our lives, and is a great place to start if you're new to reading the Bible.

Just as you saw Ariana learning in *Fire & Flood*, the support of your new family of God is super important! We encourage you to go find a Bible-centered church and tell others what you have found, so that you may be encouraged, receive guidance and discipleship, as well as give real hope to others around you.

Chapter 26
Stand Up for Truth

I. Looking at the Book:

Why do you think Nimrod would feel more powerful by holding Ariana, one of the Mothers, hostage?

Why would different thinking (or languages) be intolerable to him?

Imagine years and years of imprisonment. How does Ariana manage? How does she survive?

How does Amalthai respond to the bullying guard? Is it effective?

How does Ariana stand up against manipulation?

II. Looking at the Bible:
What does the Bible say about standing up for truth?

"Little children, let us not love with word or with tongue, but in _____ and in _____." (1 John 3:18)

While we are told to turn the other cheek, Jesus also said this to His disciples: "And He said to them, 'But now, whoever has a money belt is to take it along, likewise also a bag, and whoever has no _____ is to sell his coat and buy one'" (Luke 22:36).

Why would they need a sword?

Jesus is perfect and without sin, of course! He's our example to follow. He's described as meek or gentle. Meekness is defined as "power under control." So, while Jesus whipped the money lenders for making the house of God into a marketplace, He was exercising gentleness!

Knowing the things that were going to happen to Him, Jesus did not hide, but boldly went up to the huge crowd of hundreds of armed soldiers coming to arrest Him. Read about His bold actions in John 18:4-11.

Did He seem fearful?

How did He demonstrate His power and His love in this passage?

III. Looking at Ourselves:

What is it about bullies, that they delight in wrongdoing? How can you stand up for what's right, and yet still be loving and kind?

Do you have an example of where you've been able to do this in your own life?

"Earth is an in-between world touched by both Heaven and Hell. Earth leads directly into Heaven or directly into Hell, affording a choice between the two. The best of life on Earth is a glimpse of Heaven; the worst of life is a glimpse of Hell."
Randy Alcorn, *Heaven*

Chapter 27
Big-Picture Plan

I. Looking at the Book:
How does the King of Jordan come to believe in God?

How is the protection of God different in Jordan from the protection of the Global Union cities?

What signs do we have that Noam is not a good guy? (See page 181.)

II. Looking at the Bible:
Even though we live in a world where bad things do happen, bad things happening to us don't mean that God isn't in control or that He doesn't love us. In fact, we have God's Word that He will never leave us or forsake us!

"_____you pass through the waters, I will be with you; and through the rivers, they will not over you; _____ you walk through the fire, you will not be scorched, nor will the flame burn you." (Isaiah 43:2)

"Have I not _____ you? Be strong and _____! Do not tremble or be dismayed, for the Lord your God is _____you wherever you go." (Joshua 1:9)

"And we know that God causes _____ to work together for good to those who _____ God, to those who are _____ according to His purpose." (Romans 8:28)

III. Looking at Ourselves:

The Bible is so much more than a book of rules to obey! It's an integrated message system from a loving, Heavenly Father who wants humanity to know Him.

War was declared in the Garden of Eden by God's enemy, Satan, an angel who rebelled against the Lord ages ago. God was not surprised. He knows the "end from the beginning" and has shared His plan for the ages from Genesis to Revelation.

God has laid out His plans ahead of time to let us know where we're going in history. He reveals Himself to humanity through His Word, through the prophets, through the nation of Israel, and through His Son. Jesus shows us the Father's love in His personal involvement in our redemption.

How do you respond to God's story?

What does God tell us about this world?

What plans does He have for it?

Chapter 28
True Religion

I. Looking at the Book:

The demonstration of sensuality and nakedness is in stark contrast to Ariana and those who follow the Creator. God created the body, so why would modesty be a virtue?

What is the focus of each woman's heart?

How is it that Amalthai could be so enamored of Semiramis and Nimrod, and yet be so kind and caring?

II. Looking at the Bible:

What is the difference between a sacrifice to God, and the sacrifice made to the snake god, Marduk, in this ceremony?

"The things which the Gentiles _____, they sacrifice to _____ and not to God; and I do not want you to become sharers in _____." (1 Corinthians 10: 20)

How does God's enemy, Satan, use condescension and versions of the truth to trick people, as Akkadab did when he mockingly refers to the "so-called Flood"?

"You are of your _____the devil, and you want to do the desires of your _____. He was a _____ from the beginning and does not stand in the truth because there is _____ truth in Him. _____ he speaks a lie, he speaks from his own nature, for he is a _____ and the father of _____." (John 8:44)

*"The Bible is very clear about what we do with wolves;
we flee from them, expose them, and warn others.*
We don't pet them."
@thebereanmillennial

What is true beauty from God's perspective? (Read Proverbs 31:30 to find out.)

III. Looking at Ourselves:

Even though sometimes you feel like people might never change, God is in control. He knows what will happen and His timing is perfect. We must not give up praying for those we love to come to a believing faith in Jesus. Do not give up the faith!

For whom are you praying?

Chapter 29
Targeted but Protected

I. Looking at the Book:

It's wild to think that an unfamiliar place with so much heat, and so many people and animals, could become a home where Dani feels safe and cared for by people she trusts. What are some of the reasons she feels safe?

Why does Bellomo focus on killing the Jews?

II. Looking at the Bible:

What is God's promise to the remnant Jewish people who survive the Tribulation?

Read Zephaniah 3:12-17 and make a list of what you find there.

Why can believers ultimately feel protected during the time of the Tribulation? (See Revelation 7:9-17.)

III. Looking at Ourselves:

"The LORD your God is in your midst,
A victorious warrior.
He will rejoice over you with joy,
He will be quiet in His love,
He will rejoice over you with shouts of joy."
Zephaniah 3:17

How is God described in this passage? Does this fit with the image you have of Him? Why or why not? How does it challenge or encourage you in your thinking about the way He sees YOU?

Extra: If you enjoy drawing or painting, try creating a picture that expresses the message of this verse.

Chapter 30
Purpose and a Plan

I. Looking at the Book:

Why do you think Ariana has confidence to believe that "(God) brought me to this place with a purpose"?

Does it surprise you to read that Ariana performs a C-section on Amalthai, and had done it successfully in the past? (Note: There is evidence in the Talmud, ancient Jewish literature, that a similar procedure was in place for at-risk mothers.)

II. Looking at the Bible:

It was shocking in this chapter to see that the unusually big baby, Tammuz, spoke to Ariana.

Why do we have reason to believe that the Nephilim were still around after the Flood?

Read Genesis 6:1-8 and answer the following questions:
1. The sons of God married the daughters of men and had children with what characteristics?

2. When were the Nephilim on the earth?

Read Numbers 13:21-33. Why would Satan have had the sons of God marry women and settle in the land God promised to Abraham and his descendants, while the Jewish people were held captive in Egypt?

Read 1 Samuel 17:1-11, 31-54. How big was Goliath? (Verse 4—one cubit was 18 inches; a span was nine inches.)

Look up 2 Samuel 21:18-22. How many brothers did Goliath have?

How many stones did David take with him? What plan did David have for those stones?

III. Looking at Ourselves:

How should believers deal with biblical ideas that are challenging to understand? (See 2 Timothy 3:16.)

How can you trust and be filled with peace, even when bad things are happening? Read Philippians 4:4-7 to find some practical ways to appropriate the peace Jesus promises us.

Chapter 31

Trust

I. Looking at the Book:

What does Noam promise Dani? How is that different from what Jannik promises Dani? What motivations does each man have?

Why are both of these impossible promises?

II. Looking at the Bible:

We all make promises to others. We may have the best of intentions, but we're not always able to fulfill them. Neither of the men were able to deliver on their promises to Dani.

God's promises are different. God isn't a man. He not only has the power to fulfill everything He promises, but He also has the will to do so. Knowing God's promises to those who have trusted Jesus Christ as Savior gives us courage and a foundational assurance.

What are some of God's promises to those who have trusted Jesus? Here is just one passage from the New Testament that provides an answer: 1 Peter 1: 3-12. Verses 3-9 are below; see if you can fill in the blanks:

"Blessed (*fully satisfied*) be the God and Father of our Lord Jesus Christ, who according to His great mercy has caused us to be born again to a _____hope through the resurrection of Jesus Christ from the dead, (*God brings life from death!*) to obtain an inheritance which is imperishable and undefiled and will not fade away, _____ in heaven for you who are _____ by the power of God through faith for a salvation ready to be revealed in the _____time.

"In this you greatly rejoice, even though now for a little while, if necessary, you have been distressed by various trials, _____the proof of your faith, being more precious than gold which is perishable, even though tested by fire, may be found to result in praise and glory and honor at the _____of Jesus Christ; and though you have not seen Him, you love Him, and though you do not see Him now, but believe in Him, you greatly rejoice with joy inexpressible and full of glory, obtaining as the outcome of your faith the salvation of your souls." (1 Peter 1:3-9)

How amazing that our salvation is what fully satisfies the Father! As you read further along in the passage, you'll discover that the salvation described above is something the prophets wanted to know more about and the holy angels long to see.

III. Looking at Ourselves:

Should a person stop living because of crazy times, like Zivah suggested, as we don't know how bad things will get? Why should we live with hope and confidence?

How do we share hope with people we love?

Should we make promises about protecting them from bad things?

What should we say?

*"God's purpose in your life is not prosperity.
It is not your health. It is not wealth and more than
anything, it is not to have your best life now.
God's purpose for you as His own is to make you holy
and according to the image of Christ."*
Paul Washer

Chapter 32
When You Feel Alone

I. Looking at the Book:

Ariana is really alone again. Her only friend just died, and she is still a prisoner in an unfriendly, evil world. How does she handle her situation?

Who is really controlling Akkadab, the high priest?

How does Ariana escape from this gruesome celebration?

II. Looking at the Bible:

Sometimes it helps, when looking at Scripture, to organize phrases according to whom or what is being talked about, as shown below using the following passage:

"Blessed be the God

and Father

of our **Lord Jesus Christ**,

the Father of mercies,

and God of all _____

who _____ us in all our affliction

so that

we will be able to _____those in any affliction

with the _____

with which we are _____

by God."

(2 Corinthians 1:3-4)

How does this verse comfort you?

III. Looking at Ourselves:

It can be easy to dismiss torturous behavior, like the killing of innocent babies, as some barbaric story of history—fictional or otherwise. Why is this something we must honestly address in our society today?

Having nowhere to hide... have you ever felt like that?

Perhaps you have, like Ariana, been both afraid and angry at the same time. Describe this conflict.

What can we do when we feel like this?

How can the much-loved 23rd Psalm bring comfort and hope when we feel this way?

Psalm 23
"The Lord is my Shepherd I shall not want.
He makes me lie down in green pastures; He leads me beside
quiet waters.
He restores my soul;
He guides me in the paths of righteousness for His name's sake.
Even though I walk through the valley of the shadow of death, I
fear no evil, for You are with me;
Your rod and Your staff, they comfort me.
You prepare a table before me in the presence of my enemies;
You have anointed my head with oil; My cup overflows*
Surely goodness and loving kindness will follow me all the days
of my life, And I will dwell in the house of the LORD forever!"

*In ancient Israel, when you were a guest in someone's home for a meal, the host would pour a little wine in your cup to signal the meal was over and it was time to leave. If he wanted you to stay longer, he would fill your cup. What does it say about you that the Lord "overfills your cup"?

Chapter 33
God Speaks to Us

I.   Looking at the Book:

Who is speaking to Dani on page 220?

Does she do as she is instructed? Why or why not?

What has happened to Noam?

Noam says, "Power requires sacrifice, you know. The great one is strengthened by sacrifice, and so he strengthens us in turn." What do you think he means?

Why do you think the Global Union in New Babylon would be interested in a Propagation Institute?

II. Looking at the Bible:

> *"Satan and his evil host can do nothing the Lord does not allow them to do (Job 1-2). This being the case, Satan, thinking he is accomplishing his own purposes, is actually accomplishing God's good purposes, as in the case of Judas' betrayal. Some people develop an unhealthy fascination with the occult and demonic activity. This is unwise and unbiblical. If we pursue God, if we are clothing ourselves with His armor and relying upon His strength (Ephesians 6:10-18), we have nothing to fear from the evil ones, for God rules over all!"[7]*

Can a person be possessed by the devil or a demonic spirit? (See Matthew 10:1, 12:45; Luke 22:3.)

---

7   "What Does the Bible Say about Demon Possession?" Got Questions. Accessed July 25, 2022. https://www.gotquestions.org/demon-possession.html

In Scripture, what is always the key to relieving a person of such an affliction? Does the person need to want to be delivered?

III. Looking at Ourselves:

Have you ever been attacked with thoughts of what you should have done, and didn't do? Why is that only helpful for a short time? When does it become a destructive practice?

How can we get out of this cycle of thinking?

Chapter 34

God's Way Is Best

I. Looking at the Book:

What are Shem's reactions when he learns about what happened to Ariana while she was imprisoned?

Why does Ariana think the nursemaid, whose tongue had been cut out, went back to the city?

II. Looking at the Bible:

Read Job 42:2. Why do you think God's way is better, even if it's harder or lonelier?

Read Romans 8:31-39 and make a list of the reasons His way is better, even when we go through hard times.

How does God use difficulties to shape our character? Look at Romans 5:3-5 and list the things God wants to accomplish in our lives through difficulties. Then fill in the blanks below:

"And not only this, but we also exult in our tribulations, knowing that tribulation brings about _____; and _____, proven character; and proven character, _____; and _____ does not disappoint, because the love of God has been poured out within our hearts through the _____who was given to us."

III. Looking at Ourselves:

Why is there an attraction to return to old ways, even if they are evil or unhealthy?

How have you been tempted to return to old habits and patterns, and what strategies can you use to prevent this from happening?

Chapter 35
Women

I. Looking at the Book:
Dani punches Noam in the nose! Why and how does she get away with this?

What is the purpose of the Propagation Institute? Why would this be something Bellomo would even be concerned about?

II. Looking at the Bible:
To this day, around the world, women are enslaved: how can this be prevented from happening now and in the future?

Why does it happen?

Jesus speaks to the truth of our sinful condition apart from His salvation. Talk over the things you read about in Mark 7:20-21.

While the visible Church hasn't always lived up to God's standards regarding women, the New Testament treats women in ways that you may find surprising!

Read Mark 16: 1-11. Who was the first person to whom Jesus appeared after the resurrection?

(It is notable that, in first-century Israel, a woman could not be a witness in court, yet Jesus entrusted this woman to carry the news of His resurrection to His disciples!)

III. Looking at Ourselves:

Have you ever felt you were treated unfairly because you are a woman? How do you believe God would have you respond in a situation like that?

In this chapter, Dani wondered why bad things kept happening to her. Have *you* ever wondered, "Why does this (whatever it may be) keep happening to me?" In light of this lesson, do you think any differently now?

Chapter 36
The Real Prosperity Gospel

I. Looking at the Book:

What are some reasons why Abram might have been so quiet?

What are some examples of how God provided for all of His people in this chapter?

Was Terah's grief over Amalthai's death an excuse for his actions, sacrificing someone else's child? Why or why not?

II. Looking at the Bible:

Read Jeremiah 29:11. Does this verse appear to promise believers good things, riches, prosperity, and health here on Earth?

Now read Matthew 16:24-28. How do you reconcile what Jesus is saying to His followers with the Jeremiah 29:11 scripture? How can both be true?

Check out these verses about God's purposes for us going through trials of various kinds:

In Genesis 50:20, Joseph said that what his brothers had intended for _____, God used for _____. How does this connect to what we read in Romans 8:28-29?

III. Looking at Ourselves:

How does the fact that this world is filled with suffering hold up when you view things with God's "Big-Picture" plan?

Based on the scriptures you have read in this chapter, what do you think God wants of you?

Chapter 37
More on the Mark of the Beast

I.   Looking at the Book:

How is the mark Dani receives different from the mark of the followers of Bellomo?

Why does the female nurse, Paniz, react so violently to Dani's slow response to her call? (See *Fire & Flood*, page 247.)

Looking back, why did Mitch take the mark?

II. Looking at the Bible:

Both of the authors of this study guide believe that all of Scripture is meant to be understood—even the Book of Revelation! We follow the "golden rule" of Bible interpretation by Daniel Cooper: "When the plain sense of Scripture makes common sense, seek no other sense, lest it result in nonsense."

Many people have worried about the "mark of the beast," the number "666," and other signs mentioned in the Book of Revelation, such as the two men who will be running the show, so to speak, during the Tribulation. The first beast is described in Revelation 13:1-10.

How does the Bible describe the man known as the "Anti-Christ?"

What does he do?

Who gives him authority?

The second beast is described in Revelation 13:11-18.

What does he look like?

What does he require of the people who dwell on the earth? (v.12)

What happens to people who won't take the mark and worship the beast? (v.17)

III. Looking at Ourselves:

How hard do you think it will be during the Tribulation to resist taking the mark of the beast?

Revelation 13 takes place halfway through the Tribulation at the three-and-a-half-year mark. What preparations could you make to resist taking this mark, if this situation were to occur in your lifetime?

Here is a website with more information about the Tribulation; you may wish to check it out if you'd like to learn more: https://www.raptureready.com/

Chapter 38
Guilt

I. Looking at the Book:
"I wish the great Flood had rid us of evil, but it didn't. It's still with us." (See *Fire & Flood*, page 256.)

Why is "evil still with us"?

How do we see evidence of this reality in this chapter?

II. Looking at the Bible:
How did Adam and Eve feel after they ate the forbidden fruit? (See Genesis 3:1-7.)

How did they try to take care of their guilt?

How did God take care of their guilt? (See Genesis 3:21.)

Now that Jesus has died and risen again, how does God take care of our guilt? (See 1 John 1:9.)

III. Looking at Ourselves:

Ariana's heart is broken again, Nua dies, and Abram is taken. Ariana is wracked with guilt for leaving him unattended. How do we let feelings of guilt into our thoughts, and what do we need to do when we allow our guilt to isolate and remove us from action?

How does "hope" (or lack thereof) affect your life?

When is guilt unhealthy?

Chapter 39
True Love

I. Looking at the Book:

On page 262, Dani says, "There was nothing I could say, so I kept my mouth shut"? Do you agree with her comment?

Trace Dani's next (forced) journey on a map. Why do you think the author had Dani go to Jerusalem at this point in the story?

II. Looking at the Bible:

What is true love? (Read Romans 12:9-21.)

How is it expressed?

What the source of love? (Read 1 John 4:7-8.)

(Note: There are more words than one in Greek that are translated "love" in English. *Agape* is the Greek word used in the passage you just read. It is God's love which is the highest form. *Agape* always seeks the best for the one who is the object of love.)

III. Looking at Ourselves:

Dani wonders if Jannik would still love her if she were pregnant. If Dani was your friend, how would you reassure or comfort her?

How do you show love to people who are grieving the loss of loved ones?

Would you describe the way you love your family, friends, and neighbors as "always seeking the best" for them?

Chapter 40
Real Beauty

I. Looking at the Book:

How does this chapter suggest one deals with loss?

How does this chapter show that God was in control, that there was nothing Ariana could have done to alter or avoid Abram's capture?

"'What is your opinion of these gods (Nergal, Marduk), Abram?' asked Noah." Why do you think that was an important question to be asked of Abram?

What kinds of medicine have been commented upon since the novel began?

How did Sarai say people reacted to her infertility?

How does she deal with her pain, and how does Ariana respond appropriately?

II. Looking at the Bible:

What does the Bible say about beauty? (Read 1 Samuel 16:7 and Proverbs 31:30.)

Ariana demonstrates an admirable control over her tongue, and refrains from saying, "I just got you back. Terah doesn't deserve you."

What does the Bible say about the power of our words? (Read James 3:1-12.)

Why does the Bible say you should keep rein over your tongue, and how are you supposed to do that? (Read Psalm 34:12-13.)

III. III. Looking at Ourselves:

Whom do you know whose beauty is enhanced by a sweet nature and keen intellect? How so?

Chapter 41

Riches

I. Looking at the Book:

Despite all the riches money can buy, what evidence do you have that Matteo and Gabriella are not happy?

How does Dani respond to Matteo's suggestion?

When are flirtations dangerous?

II. Looking at the Bible:

What does the Bible say about riches? What can be dangerous about wealth? (Read Psalm 52:7.)

Will riches make you right with God? (Read Proverbs 11:4.)

What should motivate you? (Read Luke 16:13.)

Who is the one ultimately responsible for meeting our needs? (Read Philippians 4:19.)

III. Looking at Ourselves:

Surrogacy is a complicated topic, and many surrogates have given life to children to people who cannot have children of their own. What are some of the emotions all the involved parties might face in choosing this path?

Is it okay to be rich? Is it okay to be poor? Explain your answer.

"Nothing is more often misdiagnosed than our homesickness for Heaven. We think that what we want is sex, drugs, alcohol, a new job, a raise, a doctorate, a spouse, a large-screen television, a new car, a cabin in the woods, a condo in Hawaii. What we really want is the person we were made for, Jesus, and the place we were made for, Heaven. Nothing less can satisfy us."
Randy Alcorn, *Heaven*

Chapter 42
Family of God

I. Looking at the Book:

"How quickly the world turns to idols." (See *Fire & Flood,* page 281.) Why do you think this is true?

Describe the mural on the bedchamber wall, and the mosaic floor, on page 282. Why are those interesting choices for a home in Ur, a city dedicated to a variety of gods?

Who do you think made those?

II. Looking at the Bible:

"...where you go, I will go; and where you stay, I will stay" (Ruth 1:16). Similar to the Bible story of Naomi and Ruth, whose love for each other was self-sacrificing and focused on their love for God, Ariana says she has this kind of love for Abram and Sarai.

What does the Bible say about the family of God?

How does one become part of God's family? (Read John 1:12-13.)

Along with being part of the family of God, we also have a new identity. According to Ephesians 2:19, what are we called?

Read 1 John 3:1-3 and answer the following questions:

What reason did God have to make a way for us to become part of His family?

When will we truly resemble our Father? How will that happen?

Fill in the blanks from the Scripture passage: "_____, now we are children of God, and it has not appeared as yet _____ be. We know that when He appears, we will be _____, because we will see Him _____ _____."

III. Looking at Ourselves:

Have you thought about what it might be like to meet Methuselah, Noah, Abram, and Sarai?

Will time (age) matter when we get to Heaven?

Do you think you will be considered old, or young, or ageless?

Why do you think this?

Chapter 43

What Other People Think

I. Looking at the Book:

Despite all the hardships, people still rebel against the apparent strength of the Global Union and President Bellomo. Why do you think they do this, some without knowing Jesus?

What does seeing Jannik do for Dani?

Gabriella states, "We've decided to cast aside the restraints to our love, and we have you to thank for it." (See *Fire & Flood*, page 288.) What are the restraints of their love?

II. Looking at the Bible:

When did God first command mankind not to commit incest? (See Leviticus 18:6-18.)

Why do you think God did not issue that commandment sooner?

III. Looking at Ourselves:

Do you ever worry about what people assume, without having all the facts?

How has your childhood prepared you to survive/thrive among people of the world?

"We've fallen for the devil's lie. His most basic strategy, the same one he employed with Adam and Eve, is to make us believe that sin brings fulfillment. However, in reality, sin robs us of fulfillment. Sin doesn't make life interesting; it makes life empty. Sin doesn't create adventure; it blunts it. Sin doesn't expand life; it shrinks it. Sin's emptiness inevitably leads to boredom. When there's fulfillment, when there's beauty, when we see God as he truly is—an endless reservoir of fascination—boredom becomes impossible."

Randy Alcorn, *Heaven*

Chapter 44
Waiting

I. Looking at the Book:

Why doesn't everyone sense an evil presence, as Ariana does?

What is the response to Ariana's reason why she came to Ur, despite the history between her and Serug?

Is it possible to discern truth from a twisted tale? *(See Fire & Flood, page 295.)*

II. Looking at the Bible:

In the novel, how did Abram, Sarai, Terah, and Ariana escape from Ur?

How does this relate to Nehemiah 9:7-8?

What was God's purpose for Abram? (See Genesis 12: 1-3.)

Was this promise immediately fulfilled? (Read Genesis 21:1-7.)

Why would God tell Abram and Sarai that their offspring would be uncountable, offering them a sliver of hope, but then make them wait . . . and wait . . . and wait for a child?

III. Looking at Ourselves:

What is God teaching you about waiting?

What can you do while you wait that would bring you God's peace?

Chapter 45
Signs before Jesus' Second Coming

I.   Looking at the Book:
Dani sees Jannik but is returned to her prison home. What does she ask God?

What is happening outside the guest cottage? (See *Fire & Flood*, page 302.)

II.   Looking at the Bible:
What will be some of the final signs before Jesus returns again?

Luke 21: 25-32

Matthew 24:3-31

2 Peter 3:3-4

2 Timothy 3:1-5

1 Thessalonians 5:2-3

How is all of this evidence of God's great power and wrath?

III. Looking at Ourselves:

Are you ready for Jesus' return? Are you waiting eagerly?

Why or why not?

What are the most important things in your life?

Are they treasures in Heaven or on Earth?

Chapter 46
Faith and Hope

I. Looking at the Book:

What are Terah's deathbed regrets and wishes?

How are Sarai and Ariana able to trust that Abram heard from God?

How does Abram try to protect Sarai? How does he make that decision?

Can you imagine living with 300 wives and concubines? What is your immediate reaction to this cultural reality back then?

II. Looking at the Bible:

Hebrews 11 is often referred to as the "Faith Chapter" of the Bible. Looking at the examples there, what are some of the characteristics of faith?

Read 1 Peter 1:3-4. The Hebrew word for the "hope" mentioned here is *batah*, which means confidence, security, and being without care; therefore, the concept of doubt is not part of this word.

What is the basis for us to have that confidence and security? (Read John 10: 27-28.)

How does one build faith? (See Romans 10:17.)

"Therefore, Biblical hope is a reality and not a feeling. Biblical hope carries no doubt. Biblical hope is a sure foundation upon which we base our lives, believing that God always keeps His promises. Hope or confident assurance can be ours when we trust the words, "He who believes on Me has everlasting life"
(John 6:47).

Accepting that gift of eternal life means our hope is no longer filled with doubt but, rather, has at its sure foundation the whole of God's Word, the entirety of God's character, and the finished work of our Lord and Savior Jesus Christ."[8]

III. Looking at Ourselves:

Is it ever okay to keep someone safe by withholding the truth? Why or why not?

Does this limit God in any way?

Do you have the secure, unwavering knowledge that your time after you die will be spent with Jesus and His "bride," your family of God, in Heaven?

---

8   "What Does the Bible Say about Hope?" Got Questions. Accessed July 25, 2022. https://www.gotquestions.org/Bible-hope.html.

Chapter 47
I Can Only Imagine

I. Looking at the Book:

How is Daphne remembered from the first chapter? How has she changed in this one?

Why did Jesus wait to send help until Dani called?

II. Looking at the Bible:

How does God describe Jesus' return to Earth in the Second Coming?

What will that day be like? (See Revelation 19:11-16.)

III. Looking at Ourselves:

Dani saw the chaos of her life from Jesus' perspective; in each moment a comment thread appeared. "What seemed jumbled and random and hard to me had purpose because all of it was sifted through the hands of the One who now stood before me." (See *Fire & Flood*, page 317.) How does this give you peace?

How can you apply this to your own life?

The song, "I Can Only Imagine," by Bart Millard, made famous by the band Mercy Me, describes seeing Jesus face to face. How do you imagine you will respond when you first see Jesus?

If you have accepted His free gift of payment for your sins, and love Him as Lord, you can be confident that this first glimpse of Him will be filled with joy and delight!

*"For I consider that the sufferings of this present time are not worthy to be compared with **the glory** that is to be revealed to us. For the eagerly awaiting creation waits for the revealing of the **sons and daughters of God**."*
Romans 8:18-19 (emphasis added)

Chapter 48
Rescued

I. Looking at the Book:
Why do you think the book ends with the historical finish, instead of the future?

Why does Ariana respond with sarcasm to the proclamation that the pharaoh's brother is a descendant of Ham?

How have Ariana's experiences helped her to be an example and mentor to Sarai during a time of trouble?

How does the ending of the book tie the two story lines together? How are the stories similar?

Who is our ultimate Savior, to whom both of these stories point?

II. Looking at the Bible:

When our lives on this earth are over, what does the Bible say we have ahead of us? Read Revelation 21 and make some observations.

III. Looking at Ourselves:

With the knowledge that our lives on Earth are short, how should that affect the way we live?

How are your thoughts about life on Earth—and the afterlife—different (if at all) after reading *Fire & Flood* and this study guide?

"The Spirit and the bride say, "COME!"
And let the one who hears say, "COME!"
And let the one who is thirsty come;
let the one who desires, take the water of life without cost."
"He who testifies to these things says, "Yes, I am coming quickly."
Amen. Come, Lord Jesus.
Revelation 21: 17, 20 (emphasis added)

For Further Thought

What can you learn from Dani and Ariana's stories and/or the discussions and reflections you've experienced in this study, on the following themes? How might what you've learned help you live your life with better direction/focus on the Lord?

Below are some prompts of topics you might want to consider in your thinking, prayer, study, or journaling:
- Trust
- Men/Women
- Family
- Children
- Relationships
- Sex Trafficking/Rescue Organizations
- Waiting/Patience
- Discernment between Good and Evil
- God's Wrath
- Creativity
- Work
- God's Big-Picture Plan

Acknowledgments (from Dawn Morris)

In getting ready to launch *Fire & Flood*, I asked several people to join my "Launch Team." One of the women who joined our group was someone I'd never met—Lynnette Field. We share some friends in common, which is how Lynnette came to be part of our group. I met her for the first time when I delivered a copy of *Fire & Flood* to her. It was obvious to me right away that she was a kindred spirit!

The motivation for this book study was Lynnette's response to reading *Fire & Flood*. I can think of no higher compliment to an author than that a reader would be motivated to write a book study about their novel!

The Lord put it on Lynnette's heart to write an accompanying study guide. She and a team of other women worked diligently on it. As with every book, the process of editing is a tremendous amount of work. Lynnette and I worked for hours at a time, rewriting and rehashing the content.

Since *Fire & Flood* is based on Scripture from Genesis and Revelation, it was important to both Lynnette and me to include truth from the Bible that corresponds to each of the chapters of the book. We had SO much fun together, geeking out over how incredible the Bible is and what exactly we felt should be included in the book study. We truly became friends in the process of putting together the *Fire & Flood Study Guide*.

I am also indebted to my editor, Arlyn Lawrence, and her team at Inspira Literary Solutions, whose skills and expertise helped us get the *Fire & Flood Study Guide* ready for printing!

I would also like to thank Morgan James Publishing for taking on this project. The team at Morgan James is incredible, from David Hancock, the founder of Morgan James Publishing, to our author relations manager, Naomi Chellis, and everyone in between. Both Lynnette and I have appreciated working with you!

Dawn Morris

Acknowledgments (from Lynnette Field)

What joy to work with Dawn Morris on this project and celebrate how God works all things together, in unity, for those who love the Lord and are called according to His purpose (Romans 8:28-29)! I am so thankful for Dawn and appreciative of her boldness and wisdom. Dawn is the one who referred this study to her friend and editor, Arlyn Lawrence, who turned out to be a friend of many of my friends, and a fellow Canadian! Such a small world.

Many friends have supported me in ways they probably didn't even realize. Undoubtedly, I will fail to acknowledge everyone, but I would like to recognize Cindy, Bethany, Cathy, Dawn, Alyson, Kathleen, Krista, our prayer group team of Kathy and Larry, Dave and Marlys, Pam and Dale, Camile, Rachel and Jerry, and my precious children, Andrew, Madeline, and Kyle.

I will be forever grateful to my parents, Dennis and Arlene, who provided the foundations for my faith, and for the encouragement and support of my brother Randy, his wife Deanna, and children Nolan, Grace, Kenzie, and Bethany.

My greatest earthly encourager is my husband, Dwight, who believed in the idea and celebrated the purpose behind this guide every step of the way. It is an honor to be partnered with someone who loves the Lord so deeply.

Lynnette Field

About the Authors

Dawn Morris has studied the Bible for over forty years. She has taught women's Bible studies from Genesis to Revelation, as well as being a regular speaker at women's retreats and prophecy conferences. She holds a bachelor's degree in Elementary Education from the University of Houston, and is the author of three novels: *One Will Be Taken, One Will Be Left*, and *Fire & Flood*. She is currently working on her fourth novel, *One Will Stand*, and a devotional, *Twenty-Three Doors: My Journey with Jesus*.

Dawn lives in the beautiful Pacific Northwest in Washington State with her husband, three dogs, and three cats. Dawn and Dennis have five grown children, one of whom is waiting for them in Heaven.

www.dawn-morris.com

Lynnette Field is an excellence-driven educator with experience teaching almost every subject imaginable in both public and private schools. She has passionately taught elementary, middle, and high school for over three decades. Lynnette has taught Bible studies to women of all ages.

Lynnette attended the Baptist Leadership Training School in Calgary, Alberta, and shortly thereafter earned a bachelor's degree in Education from the University of British Columbia. Lynnette and her husband, Dwight, are avid hikers and campers and they reside in Gig Harbor, Washington. Together they have two grown sons, a daughter-in-law, and several beloved pets.

Resources

Abortion/Life of Unborn
* https://www.focusonthefamily.com/pro-life/what-the-bible-says-about-the-beginning-of-life/

Angels
* https://www.gotquestions.org/angels-Bible.html

Antichrist
* Matthew 24: 5,24
* Mark 13: 6, 22
* 2 Thessalonians 2: 3-12
* 1 John 2: 18-22, 4: 1-3
* 2 John 1:7

Apologetics (Proving Evidence for Christ)
* *More Than A Carpenter* (easy to read) and/or
* *Evidence That Demands A Verdict* (more in-depth), both by Josh McDowell
* *The Case for Christ* by Lee Stroebel (book, DVD)

- *God's Not Dead*, (1, 2, & 3) movies available through Pure Flix or Christianbook.com
- *Defending Your Faith* by R.C. Sproul

Biblical Historical Evidence:
- AnswersinGenesis.org
- https://www.cslewisinstitute.org/webfm_send/410
- https://www.blueletterbible.org/Comm/stewart_don/faq/bible-authoritative-word/question2-is-the-bible-the-inspired-word-of-god.cfm

Caesarean Sections in History:
- https://earlychurchhistory.org/medicine/c-sections-in-the-ancient-world/
- http://www.talmudology.com/jeremybrownmdgmailcom/2019/8/26/keritot-7b-surviving-a-cesarian-section-j6zds

Cults
- https://dwellcc.org/learning/essays/christian-cults-and-sects

Discerning False Prophets
- https://www.thegospelcoalition.org/article/7-traits-of-false-teachers/
- https://bereanresearch.org/
- Video: *American Gospel: Christ Alone* (Full two-hour or one-hour version on Pure Flix,
- YouTube, or Netflix)
- Books:
- *The Way of the Dragon or the Way of the Lamb: Searching for Jesus' Path of Power in a Church that Has Abandoned It* by Jamin Goggin and Kyle Stroebel
- *Defining Deception* by Anthony Wood and Costi Hinn

Giants/Nephilim

- https://smile.amazon.com/Giants-Record-Americas-History-Smithsonian/dp/0956786510/ref=sr_1_2?crid=25ZHBFCVBSYQD&dchild=1&keywords=jim+viera&qid=1630626366&sprefix=jim+vier%2Cdigital-text%2C205&sr=8-2
- https://answersingenesis.org/bible-characters/who-were-the-nephilim/
- *(This discusses the various Christian views, showing that Dawn Morris' beliefs hold to the most popular thinking: although Mr. Bode does not come to the same conclusion as the author, he opens up discussion points.)*
- John MacArthur's research: https://www.gty.org/library/sermons-library/90-254/demonic-invasion

God's Overall Plan

- http://www.elegantfarmer.com/wp-content/uploads/2014/08/GODS-OVERALL-PLAN.pdf

Heaven:

- *Heaven* by Randy Alcorn
- *The Case for Heaven* by Lee Strobel

Human Trafficking (Organizations Working to End Trafficking):

- Adorned/Compassion Washington (compassionwa.com)
- Rattanak International, Burnaby, B.C., Canada

Israel

- https://metrovoicenews.com/in-videos-franklin-graham-and-daughter-explore-why-israel-matters/
- https://www.christianbook.com/jerusalem-biblical-historical-case-jewish-capital/jay-sekulow/9781640880771/pd/880772?event=PRCBD1#CBD-PD-Description

Kinsman-Redeemer

- https://www.gotquestions.org/kinsman-redeemer.html

Maps

- You may wish to look up maps of Bible lands, and of the USA, Canada, and other world locations, that illustrate the places where Dani and Ariana's stories take place. Some recommended sites for these are:
- https://bible-history.com/maps/
- https://www.nationsonline.org/oneworld/map/world_map.htm

Rapture

- https://www.focusonthefamily.com/family-qa/what-the-bible-has-to-say-about-the-rapture/
- https://www.gty.org/library/topical-series-library/222/the-rapture-and-the-day-of-the-lord
- https://www.moodybible.org/beliefs/positional-statements/second-coming/
- Book Resource: *Because the Time Is Near* by John MacArthur

https://www.raptureready.com/

Resisting Satan/Evil

- https://www.desiringgod.org/articles/satans-ten-strategies-against-you

Sharing Your Faith

- https://www.bereanmn.com/berean-blog/its-a-beautiful-day-in-the-neighborhood-to-tell-others-about-jesus/

Technology in Ancient Times

Authors' Note: There is a lot of evidence that the Pre-Flood world had more refinements in technology and culture than we think. Exodus 31:3, 35:31-35 credits the Spirit of God with giving craftsmen, stone cutters, wood workers, engravers, designers, embroiderers, and others the understanding and skills they needed.

Theology (Positional Guidance)

- Book: *Systematic Theology: An Introduction to Biblical Doctrine,* by Wayne Grudem
- https://www.christianbook.com/systematic-theology -introduction-to-biblical-doctrine/wayne-grudem/9780310286707/pd/28670?event=AFF&p=1155287&

Women

- https://www.gotquestions.org/womens-rights.html

Appendix

Map of Babylon/ Ancient Biblical Times
Including Tigris and Euphrates Rivers [9]

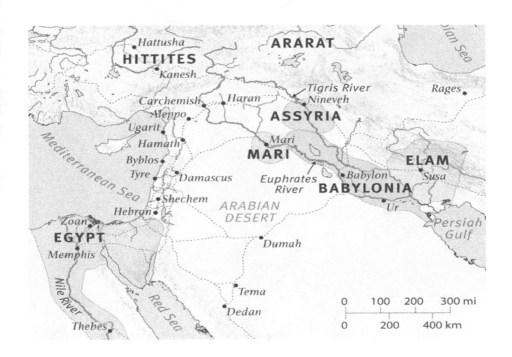

9   https://www.bible.ca/maps/maps-near-east-abrahams-journey.jpg

Lifespan Overlap of Early Figures in the Bible[10]

Comparative Lifespan Chart, Adam to Abram

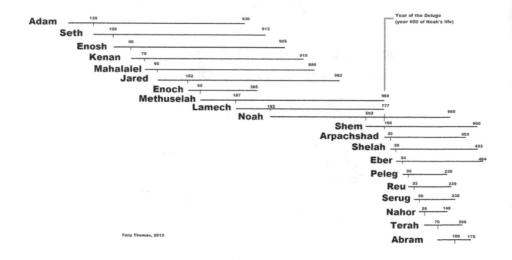

Tony Thomas, 2013

10   Hodge, Bodie. "Methuselah: When Did He Die?" Answers in Genesis. July 30, 2010. https://answersingenesis.org/bible-timeline/genealogy/when-did-methuselah-die/

A free ebook edition is available with the purchase of this book.

To claim your free ebook edition:

1. Visit MorganJamesBOGO.com
2. Sign your name CLEARLY in the space
3. Complete the form and submit a photo of the entire copyright page
4. You or your friend can download the ebook to your preferred device

Morgan James
BOGO™

A **FREE** ebook edition is available for you
or a friend with the purchase of this print book.

CLEARLY SIGN YOUR NAME ABOVE

Instructions to claim your free ebook edition:
1. Visit MorganJamesBOGO.com
2. Sign your name CLEARLY in the space above
3. Complete the form and submit a photo
   of this entire page
4. You or your friend can download the ebook
   to your preferred device

Print & Digital Together Forever.

Snap a photo

Free ebook

Read anywhere

CPSIA information can be obtained
at www.ICGtesting.com
Printed in the USA
JSHW080001081022
31438JS00001B/20

9 781636 980195